DISCOVER AMERICA

MINNESOTA

Neil Purslow

AV² provides enriched content that supplements and complements this book. Weigl's AV² books strive to create inspired learning and engage young minds in a total learning experience.

Your AV² Media Enhanced books come alive with...

Audio
Listen to sections of the book read aloud.

Key Words
Study vocabulary, and complete a matching word activity.

Video
Watch informative video clips.

Quizzes
Test your knowledge.

Embedded Weblinks
Gain additional information for research.

Slide Show
View images and captions, and prepare a presentation.

Try This!
Complete activities and hands-on experiments.

... and much, much more!

Go to www.av2books.com, and enter this book's unique code.

BOOK CODE

H 8 6 3 2 4 7

AV² by Weigl brings you media enhanced books that support active learning.

Published by AV² by Weigl
350 5th Avenue, 59th Floor
New York, NY 10118
Website: www.av2books.com

Library of Congress Cataloging-in-Publication Data
Names: Purslow, Neil, author.
Title: Minnesota : the North Star State / Neil Purslow.
Description: New York, NY : AV2 by Weigl, [2016] | Series: Discover America |
  Includes index.
Identifiers: LCCN 2015048020 (print) | LCCN 2015048324 (ebook) | ISBN
  9781489648846 (hard cover : alk. paper) | ISBN 9781489648853 (soft cover :
  alk. paper) | ISBN 9781489648860 (Multi-User eBook)
Subjects: LCSH: Minnesota--Juvenile literature.
Classification: LCC F606.3 .P875 2016 (print) | LCC F606.3 (ebook) | DDC 977.6--dc23
LC record available at http://lccn.loc.gov/2015048020

Printed in the United States of America, in Brainerd, Minnesota
1 2 3 4 5 6 7 8 9 20 19 18 17 16

042016
220416

Project Coordinator Heather Kissock
Art Director Terry Paulhus

Photo Credits
Every reasonable effort has been made to trace ownership and to obtain permission to reprint copyright material. The publisher would be pleased to have any errors or omissions brought to their attention so that they may be corrected in subsequent printings. The publisher acknowledges Getty Images, Corbis Images, and Alamy as its primary image suppliers for this title.

MINNESOTA

Contents

STATE TREE
Red or Norway Pine

STATE BIRD
Common Loon

STATE FLAG
Minnesota

STATE FLOWER
Pink and White Lady's Slipper

STATE FISH
Walleye

STATE SEAL
Minnesota

Nickname
The North Star State

Motto
L'Etoile du Nord
(The Star of the North)

Song
"Hail Minnesota" by Truman E.
Rickard and Arthur E. Upson

Population
(2014 Census) 5,457,173
Ranked 21st state

Entered the Union
May 11, 1858, as the 32nd state

Capital
St. Paul

Discover Minnesota

Minnesota is famous for its many lakes. One of the state's nicknames is Land of 10,000 Lakes, but there are actually more than 12,000. With so many lakes, fishing and canoeing are popular recreational sports. Along Minnesota's lakeshores are a variety of cabins, beaches, tourist camps, and resorts. In addition to its lakes, the state's plentiful resources include rivers, forests, minerals, and fertile soil. These resources have allowed a diverse economy to evolve over the years. Today, food processing, particularly of corn and dairy products, and other manufacturing contribute greatly to the state's wealth.

The natural landscape of Minnesota is etched with valleys, prairies, wilderness areas, high bluffs, and rocky shores. Minnesota borders Wisconsin to the east, Iowa to the south, and the Dakotas to the west. Bordering Canada to the north, the state extends farther north than any other state in the country except Alaska.

About one out of every two Minnesotans lives within the greater **metropolitan area** of Minneapolis and St. Paul, which together are known as the Twin Cities. These neighboring cities straddle the Mississippi River. Minneapolis, which means "city of water," is known for its clean, modern look and its beautiful lakes and parks. The state's largest city, it has 16 lakes as well as lagoons, other wetlands, and more than 150 parks within its limits.

The Land

Lake Itasca, in northwest Minnesota, is the source of the **Mississippi River**. The lake is located in Itasca State Park.

Minnesota has *MORE SHORELINE* than Hawaii, Florida, and California combined, at nearly *90,000 MILES*.

The Mississippi River is the third longest river in North America. It stretches 2,350 miles.

Homesteaders made their way into Minnesota after 1803. Family groups would clear land and use the timber for fuel and to build homes.

Beginnings

There is evidence of prehistoric people being in the area of Minnesota as far back as 5,000 years ago. At one time, a group called Moundbuilders built more than 10,000 mounds all over the state. They were used as both ceremonial burial sites and as homes for those with a higher status within the community. The first Native American groups to make their home in Minnesota were the Sioux, Ojibwa, and Winnebago.

In 1660, French fur traders from Canada explored the area now known as Minnesota. Eventually, the British explorer Jonathan Carver made his way up the Mississippi into Minnesota in 1766, and spent time living with the Sioux people. It was not until after the Louisiana purchase in 1803 that settlers began exploring the area and bigger settlements were established.

Fur traders were the first true settlers to the area. The first settlement was called Mendota. This village became a fur trading center as well as the home of the first Minnesota governor, Henry Sibley.

Where is MINNESOTA?

Minnesota's largest cities are located in the eastern part of the state. These include Minneapolis, St. Paul, and Bloomington. The northern part of the state is much less densely populated than the southern part. The state has more than 6,500 rivers and streams. In addition to the Mississippi River, other notable waterways include the Red River of the North, on the western border, the St. Croix River, on the east, and the Minnesota River.

NORTH DAKOTA

SOUTH DAKOTA

United States Map

Minnesota

Alaska Hawai'i

MAP LEGEND

- ◼ Minnesota
- ☆ Capital City
- ● Major City
- ⌇ Mississippi River
- ▲ Mississippi River Recreation Area
- ◖ Voyageurs National Park
- ◼ Canada
- ◻ Bordering States
- ◻ Water

N

SCALE 0 ———— 50 miles

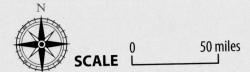

1 St. Paul

When the Minnesota Territory was organized in 1849, St. Paul became the territorial capital. Minnesota was granted statehood in 1858. That same year, St. Paul became the state capital. The city sits along the Mississippi River and has more shoreline than any other city in the United States.

2 Bloomington

Bloomington is the fourth-largest city in Minnesota. It is also home to the largest enclosed shopping mall in the United States, the Mall of America. The mall is big enough to house 32 Boeing 747 airplanes. The city is an economic hub, with several companies headquartered in the city, including Wells Fargo Bank.

CANADA

Lake Superior

4

WISCONSIN

3

St. Paul

Bloomington

1

2

Mississippi River

MINNESOTA

---

3 ## Mississippi River Recreation Area

Between Minneapolis and St. Paul runs the Mississippi River. Visitors can experience a 72-mile river park that also runs through the two cities and beyond. The recreation area offers boating, fishing, and other activities along the banks of the great Mississippi River.

4 ## Voyageurs National Park

Voyageurs National Park is a pristine wilderness area that combines natural beauty with history and encompasses more than 340 square miles of land. The remote areas of the park are accessed mainly by water or air, and offer popular attractions such as canoeing, boating, fishing, and other outdoor activities.

Land Features

Minnesota is made up of two major natural regions. In the northeastern corner is the Superior Upland. This region is a forested area of lakes, peat **bogs**, and ridges. Long ago, **glaciers** scraped away most of the soil in this part of the state.

The other major land region in Minnesota is the Central Lowland. It covers the largest part of the state. This area was sculpted by glaciers and is generally flat, with some hills and valleys. All of this portion of Minnesota was once the floor of prehistoric Lake Agassiz.

Nerstrand-Big Woods State Park

This state park, which contains the Hidden Falls Waterfall, is on the site of the Big Woods, a vast stretch of trees that settlers found when they arrived in the 1850s.

Superior Upland

The Superior Upland, in the northeastern part of Minnesota, contains valuable beds of iron ore beneath the land's surface.

Lake Superior

Lake Superior makes up Minnesota's northeast border. The lakeshore is characterized by rugged cliffs, rock-filled pools, woods, and waterfalls.

Central Lowland

Much of the Central Lowland is a fertile plain with rolling prairie, hills, and valleys.

Climate

Minnesota's climate tends to be extreme. Warm summer temperatures average 70° Fahrenheit in the southern part of the state, and cold winter readings hover around 6°F in the north. The thermometer plunges to subzero temperatures during cold snaps in winter, with the coldest temperature recorded on February 2, 1996, reaching –60°F, set near the city of Tower. On the other hand, heat waves are common occurrences in summer, with the hottest temperatures on record set at Beardsley on July 29, 1917, and at Moorhead on July 6, 1936, both reaching upwards of 114°F. The average annual precipitation ranges from 34 inches in the southeast to only 19 inches in the northwest.

Average Annual Precipitation Across Minnesota

The average annual precipitation varies for different cities across Minnesota. Why might Grand Meadow get so much more rainfall than Karlstad?

LEGEND

Average Annual Precipitation (in inches) 1961–1990

200 – 100.1

100 – 25.1

25 – 5 and less

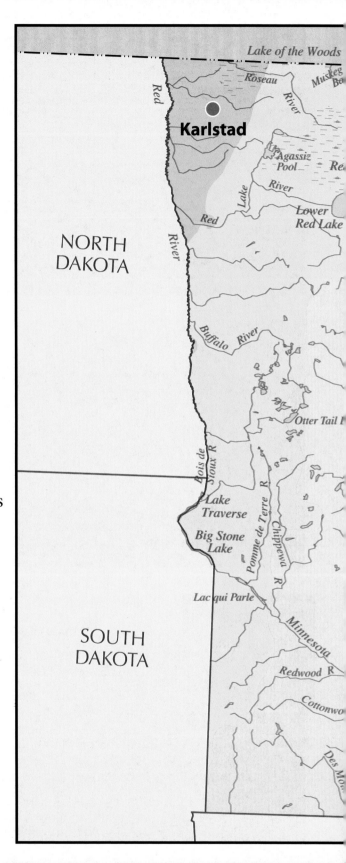

CANADA

ONTARIO

N

Rainy

Rainy Lake

Kabetogama
Lake

Little Fork River

Big Fork R

Vermilion
Lake

Lake
Winnibigoshish

Prairie R

Cloquet R

Lake Superior

Leech
Lake

St. Louis

Big Sandy
Lake

St. Louis R

MICHIGAN

Crow Wing

Gull
Lake

R

Mille Lacs
Lake

St Croix River

Mississippi

Rum

River

WISCONSIN

Crow R

Lake
Minnetonka

Crow

River

River

Cannon

River

R

Root R

Blue Earth R

● **Grand Meadow**

The Mesabi Range is the largest of three iron ranges in Minnesota.

Nature's Resources

Minnesota sits on huge reserves of iron ore, a mineral used to make steel. The iron ore is mined from both underground mines and **open-pit mines**, near the surface. These mines account for about 90 percent of the state's total mineral income. Minnesota is the largest producer of iron ore in the United States.

Long ago, two-thirds of the state was covered with needle-leaf and hardwood forests. During the 1800s, the lumber industry was a central part of the state's economy. The forests were extensively logged and cleared for farms, however, and production fell off in the early 1900s. Today, only about one-third of Minnesota is still covered in forest. Most of the wood harvested by the state's forest industries is used to make wood products or to produce pulp and paper.

Mining iron ore contributes $1.8 billion to the state's economy.

Today, loggers harvest about 3.2 billion cubic feet of wood annually.

Vegetation

Coniferous forests once covered the northeastern third of the state. Logging in the region in the 1800s removed huge amounts of valuable pine from the area's coniferous forests. The regrowth of the forests included birch, poplar, and other trees. Two-thirds of the land consisted mainly of **deciduous forests** and tall-grass prairie. When settlers from other parts of the United States arrived in what is now Minnesota, they turned much of the prairies into farms.

A belt of deciduous forest known as the Big Woods still extends from the southeastern part of the state to the Canadian border. Oak, maple, and basswood grow in this forest. Ash, elm, cottonwood, and box elder grow along the forest's stream valleys.

Minnesota has many beautiful wildflowers. They include the blue-eyed grass, pasqueflower, blazing star, and Northern blue flag. Prairie lilies, coneflowers, and pasture roses grow on the state's prairies.

Clustered Black Snakeroot

This yellow wild flower is native to Minnesota. It blooms June through July and is found mostly in the southeast part of the state.

Blue Beech

The blue beech is a small, slow growing tree native to Minnesota. It is named for its blue-gray bark.

Wild Rice

The wild rice plant grows in shallow bodies of water. It produces a nutty-flavored seed eaten by both people and waterfowl.

Pasqueflower

This wildflower is one of the first flowers that blooms in the spring on the Minnesota prairies.

Wildlife

Minnesota's northern forests are home to black bears, timber wolves, moose, and other large mammals. White-tailed deer are very common. Smaller mammals such as raccoons, woodchucks, muskrats, mink, and skunks also live throughout the state. Common birds in the state include the cardinal, goldfinch, bluebird, and a small songbird called the white-breasted nuthatch. In recent years, Minnesota has seen an increase in the population of several types of birds that had been becoming more scarce. These include the wild turkey, tundra swan, trumpeter swan, sandhill crane, bald eagle, and peregrine falcon.

There are 14 **species** of frogs and toads in Minnesota. The gray treefrog is often spotted near swamps and wetlands containing flooded trees and shrubs. Seven species of salamanders call the state their home, including the spotted and tiger varieties. Only two venomous snakes can be found in the state, the massasauga and the timber rattlesnakes.

Monarch Butterfly

The monarch butterfly is Minnesota's state butterfly. It spends the summer in Minnesota, and then travels south to find a warmer home during the winter.

Black Bear

The black bear is the largest mammal in Minnesota. An adult male can weigh up to 500 pounds.

Woodchuck

Woodchucks are found in both rural and urban areas. They eat a variety of vegetables, grasses, and legumes.

Double-crested Cormorant

There are more than 15,000 nesting pairs of cormorants in Minnesota. This native species eats 1 to 1.5 pounds of fish a day.

Economy

Grand Portage National Monument

Grand Portage National Monument is a reconstructed trading post in the northeastern corner of the state. Park staff and volunteers dress in period costume and teach visitors about what life was like at the old post.

Tourism

Minnesota's lakes, cabins, and summer weather bring tourists from all over the United States. Many come for the recreational activities, such as boating, fishing, and swimming. The Winterfest in Duluth, the Winter Carnival in St. Paul, and the John Beargrease Sled Dog Marathon draw crowds in winter. The marathon is a 390-mile dogsled race from Duluth to the north shore of Lake Superior and back.

One of the largest national forests in the United States is Superior National Forest, in the northeastern part of Minnesota. This forest includes Winnibigoshish, Leech, and Cass lakes. Minnesota also has 66 state parks, six state recreation areas, and eight scenic waysides.

Water Park of America

Water Park of America is the tallest indoor water park in the United States. It houses the tallest indoor waterslide in the country, standing at more than 100 feet tall. The waterpark is located inside the Mall of America in Bloomington, Minnesota.

Mall of America

The Mall of America, in Bloomington, is the nation's largest retail and entertainment complex. It contains a large indoor amusement park, an aquarium, a golf course, and more than 500 stores.

Minneapolis Sculpture Garden

The Minneapolis Sculpture Garden is one of the largest urban sculpture gardens in the United States. Its centerpiece is Spoonbridge and Cherry, a piece created by Claes Oldenburg and Coosje van Bruggen in the 1980s.

There are 47 millions chickens raised on Minnesota farms every year.

Primary Industries

Wheat once dominated Minnesota's agricultural economy. Although wheat is still grown in Minnesota, corn and dairy farming have replaced it in importance. Corn is produced primarily as feed for pigs and cows. Dairy farms are found in the hilly southeastern and central portions of the state. Other leading farm products in Minnesota include soybeans, hay, sugar beets, potatoes, barley, hogs, cattle, chickens, and sheep.

Manufacturing is another important part of the state's economy. Food processing and the manufacture of machinery and high-technology equipment are all prominent. The state's food-processing industries pack meat, process dairy products, mill grain, and package fruits and vegetables.

One of the state's best-known companies is 3M, which began in 1902 as the Minnesota Mining and Manufacturing Company. The company, which has its headquarters in St. Paul, makes a wide range of products, including adhesive tape, photographic film, electronics and medical materials, and Post-It brand notepads. General Mills, headquartered in Golden Valley, is a major producer of cereal and other food products.

Minneapolis was once known as the **Mill City** for its large number of **flour mills**.

The sugar beet industry generates nearly **$5 billion** for Minnesota's economy each year.

Value of Goods and Services (in Millions of Dollars)

While manufacturing is important in Minnesota, the area of finance, insurance, and real estate contributes more to the state's economy. Other types of service industries, which provide services for people rather than actual products, are also important to the state's economy. What types of services are provided by the health-care industry and the people who work in it?

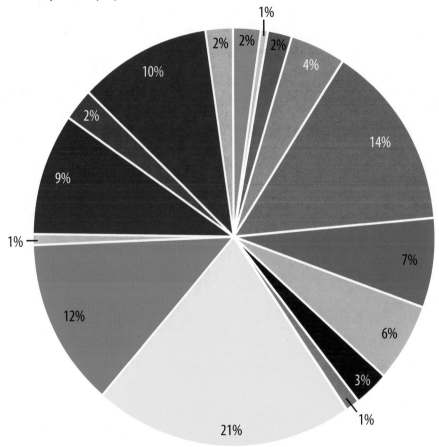

Agriculture	$6,941	Media and Entertainment	$3,131
Mining	$2,326	Finance, Insurance, and Real Estate	$63,610
Utilities	$5,341	Professional and Business Services	$39,603
Construction	$13,529	Education	$2,943
Manufacturing	$43,907	Health Care and Social Services	$28,810
Wholesale Trade	$21,849	Hotels and Restaurants	$7,514
Retail Trade	$17,931	Government	$31,672
Transportation and Warehousing	$9,041	Other Services	$6,724

In 2014, dairy farmers in Minnesota made about $1,200 per cow.

Goods and Services

The varied service sector of the economy employs the majority of all workers in the state. Minnesota's tourism industry also employs many workers in hotels and restaurants. Computer-related services and other high-technology industries have become increasingly important to the state economy, including the manufacturing of computers, office equipment, electronics, and electronic equipment.

With such a strong agricultural sector, Minnesota farmers have long formed **cooperatives** to help buy and sell their products. Today, the largest and most important consumer cooperatives in the state are the creameries. The creameries sell dairy products such as milk, butter, and cheese.

Minnesota has nearly 300,000 manufacturing jobs available across the state. These include the manufacturing of computers and electronics, metal products, and machinery.

Rivers were the first important mode for transporting people and goods in many parts of the state. **Barges** on the Mississippi River carry bulk products to and from the major inland ports at St. Paul and Minneapolis. The rail system of northeastern Minnesota brings iron ore and taconite products to the Lake Superior ports of Duluth and Superior, Wisconsin.

Nearly 7 percent of grain exports out of Minnesota are carried by barge.

History

The Ojibwe are the third-largest Native American group in the U.S. today.

The Dakota, or Sioux, lived in large buffalo-hide tents, called tipis. They were designed to be put up and taken down quickly. An entire village could be packed up and ready to move within an hour.

Native Americans

By the late 1600s, the Ojibwe, also called Chippewa, **migrated** into what is now Minnesota. The Dakota, also called Sioux, were already living around the Lake Superior region. The Ojibwe settled in the forest regions of northern and central Minnesota. They drove the Dakota into the prairies of the southern and western areas, and settled in permanent villages of dome-shaped houses. The women tended small gardens and gathered wild plants, while the men hunted and fished.

Settlers began moving into the area in the mid-1800s, and they wanted the Native Americans' land. Both the Dakota and Ojibwe were forced to sign treaties that gave most of their land in Minnesota to the United States. The United States did not keep most of the promises made to the Native Americans in the treaties.

In 1862, the Dakota rose up against the settlers in the Minnesota River Valley because of disagreements over land rights and the unfair treatment of Native Americans in the area. Today, most of the Ojibwe in Minnesota live in the Twin Cities area or on one of seven reservations in the north. The state's Dakota live mainly in four communities in the south.

Exploring the Land

In 1660, French fur traders Pierre Esprit Radisson and Médard Chouart, sieur des Groseilliers, were the first Europeans to visit what is now Minnesota. They explored the western portion of the Lake Superior area. In 1673, French explorers Father Jacques Marquette and Louis Joliet traveled to the upper portion of the Mississippi River. Six years later, Daniel Greysolon, sieur du Lhut, entered the area by way of Lake Superior. He spent time with the Dakota near Mille Lacs and claimed much of what is now Minnesota for France. Later, the city of Duluth took its name from du Lhut.

Timeline of Settlement

1679 Daniel Greysolon, sieur du Lhut, enters the area and spends time with the Dakota near Mille Lacs.

1680 Father Louis Hennepin explores the upper Mississippi River.

Settlements and U.S. Control

1673 Jacques Marquette and Louis Joliet traveled the upper portion of the Mississippi River.

1727 Fort Beauharnois is built on the shore of Lake Pepin.

1660 French fur traders Pierre Esprit Radisson and Médard Chouart, sieur des Groseilliers, become the first Europeans to visit the area.

1783 After the American Revolutionary War, the United States gains what is now northeastern Minnesota from Great Britain.

Early Exploration

Father Louis Hennepin was a French missionary sent to explore the upper Mississippi River. In 1680, he discovered and named St. Anthony Falls. Soon after Hennepin's discovery, the area became a favorite hunting ground for French fur traders. Hennepin, meanwhile, was captured by the Dakota and had to be rescued by Daniel Greysolon.

Fur trader René Boucher traveled to Minnesota in 1727 with a team of explorers. His expedition eventually arrived on the shore of Lake Pepin. A fort was built on the site and became known as Fort Beauharnois.

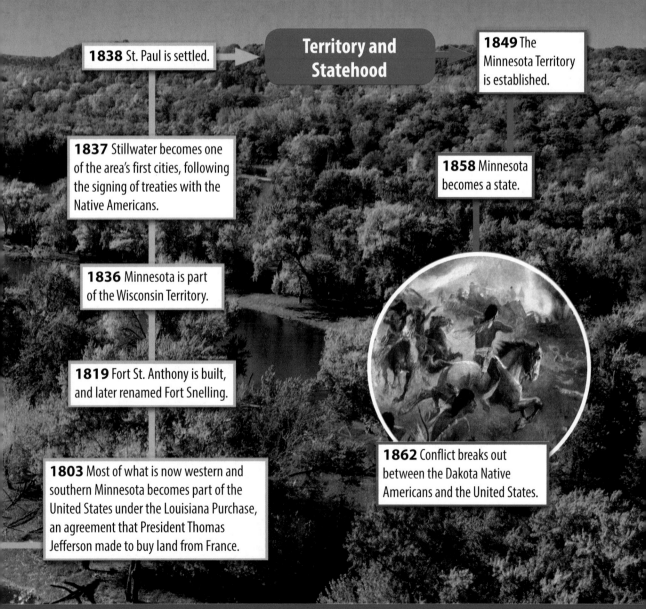

1838 St. Paul is settled.

Territory and Statehood

1849 The Minnesota Territory is established.

1837 Stillwater becomes one of the area's first cities, following the signing of treaties with the Native Americans.

1858 Minnesota becomes a state.

1836 Minnesota is part of the Wisconsin Territory.

1819 Fort St. Anthony is built, and later renamed Fort Snelling.

1862 Conflict breaks out between the Dakota Native Americans and the United States.

1803 Most of what is now western and southern Minnesota becomes part of the United States under the Louisiana Purchase, an agreement that President Thomas Jefferson made to buy land from France.

Fort Snelling sits at the junction of the Minnesota and Mississippi Rivers.

The First Settlers

The first permanent U.S. settlement in the region that became Minnesota was Fort St. Anthony, which was established in 1819. A few years later, it was renamed Fort Snelling in honor of Colonel Josiah Snelling, who built it. Settlement in the area grew in the years that followed.

During the middle of the 1800s, the U.S. government signed several treaties with Native American groups, which turned over most of the Native Americans' land to the United States. Settlers then flocked to the Mississippi and Minnesota River valleys to farm the fertile soil. In 1858, Minnesota became a state.

The Great Northern Railway competed with the Northern Pacific. It ran from St. Paul, Minnesota, to Seattle, Washington.

Another rapid period of settlement in Minnesota occurred during the 1880s, when settlers rushed to claim land in the western and southwestern parts of the state. In the same period, lumbering was at its peak, and **flour milling** was becoming important. Both Minneapolis and the neighboring city of St. Paul tripled in population during the 1880s.

In 1875, logging in Minnesota was booming. However, by 1929, the forest was depleted.

Minneapolis was the state's lumber, milling, and retail center. St. Paul was the center of transportation, wholesaling, finance, and government. Railroads played a key role in the growth of these Twin Cities. In 1883, a great celebration marked the completion of the Northern Pacific Railway from St. Paul to the West Coast.

St. Paul's growth was completely dependent on Fort Snelling. The city grew from the demands of the military men stationed at the fort.

History Makers

Many notable Minnesotans contributed to the development of their state and country. While no U.S. presidents have come from the state, a number of vice presidents, Supreme Court justices, and other leaders have called Minnesota home. Minnesotans also like to claim the legendary folk hero Paul Bunyan as their own.

William O. Douglas (1898–1980)

William O. Douglas was born in Maine Township. In the 1930s, he became one of President Franklin D. Roosevelt's advisers, and in 1939, he became a justice on the U.S. Supreme Court. During his time as a justice, Douglas was a strong defender of personal freedom and **First Amendment** rights. He retired from the Court in 1975. Douglas served on the Court for 36 years and 209 days, making him the longest serving justice in Supreme Court history.

Harry Blackmun (1908–1999)

Harry Blackmun was born in Illinois and raised in St. Paul, Minnesota. After attending Harvard Law School, Blackmun became a lawyer and then was named to the U.S. Supreme Court in 1970. Blackmun is known for writing the Court's opinion on the ruling of Roe V. Wade, which dealt with an important women's health issue. He retired from the court in 1994.

Toni Stone (1921–1996)

Born in St. Paul, Minnesota, Toni Stone started playing baseball when she was just 10 years old. By the time she was 15, Stone was seen as a phenomenon in the baseball world. In 1953, she became the first woman to play professional baseball when she was signed by the Indianapolis Clowns of the Negro Leagues.

Walter Mondale (1928–)

Walter Mondale was born in Ceylon. He graduated from the University of Minnesota Law School. In 1964, he became a U.S. senator from Minnesota. In January 1977, he became U.S. vice president under Jimmy Carter. Mondale ran for the presidency in 1984 but was defeated by Ronald Reagan.

Catharine MacKinnon (1946–)

Catharine MacKinnon was born in Minneapolis, Minnesota, in 1946. After graduating from Yale Law School, she began a career as a women's activist. Catharine fought to hold companies accountable for workplace harrassment based on gender.

Culture

About 48 percent of Minnesota residents have some college education. This is the second highest percentage in the United States.

The People Today

More than 70 percent of Minnesotans live in towns or cities. The Twin Cities and their suburbs make up the major population center of the state, with about half of the state's residents living in the area. Duluth, Rochester, and St. Cloud are the main population centers outside the Twin Cities.

St. Paul is known as "the city of neighborhoods" and offers residents a diverse place to live and work.

The vast majority of Minnesota's population is made up of people of European descent. About 4.7 percent of people in the state are African American, 4.3 percent are Hispanic, 3.8 percent are Asian, and 1.3 percent are Native American. Most of the Native Americans in Minnesota are Ojibwe.

There are more than 2,000 public schools in Minnesota, with about 55,000 full-time teachers. Nearly 842,000 students are enrolled in grades kindergarten through 12 in the state. More than 92 percent of people in Minnesota, age 25 and over, have graduated from high school. About 32 percent of people in the state, age 25 and over, have a bachelor's degree or higher.

Minnesota's state college and university system is made up of 25 two-year colleges and seven state universities. The main University of Minnesota campus is in the Twin Cities. There are also private educational institutions in the state, such as Carlton College and St. Olaf College, both located in Northfield, and Macalester College, in St. Paul.

Minnesota's population has grown every decade since 1950 and is now more than **75 percent** larger than in the mid-twentieth century.

Q What kind of actions does a state need to take to deal with this type of population growth?

The marble dome of the Minnesota capitol building is the second-largest in the world.

State Government

In 1857, a convention was held to draw up a constitution for the state. The Democratic and Republican parties were so divided that they drafted separate constitutions. After weeks of debate, they finally reached an agreement. Voters approved the new constitution that year.

The state government is divided into three branches. They are the executive, the legislative, and the judicial. The executive branch, led by the governor, is responsible for making sure the laws are carried out. The legislative branch is made up of two parts, the Senate and the House of Representatives. The legislative branch creates new laws and changes existing ones. The judicial branch consists of the state's courts.

Mark Dayton is the 40th governor of Minnesota. He has been serving since 2011.

A mural featuring Lady Minnesota is displayed in the House of Representatives Chamber. On her left is a settler, and on her right is a Native American.

Minnesota's state song is called **"Hail Minnesota."**

Minnesota, hail to thee! Hail to thee our state so dear! Thy light shall ever be

A beacon bright and clear. Thy sons and daughters true Will proclaim thee near and far.

They shall guard thy fame And adore thy name;

Thou shalt be their Northern Star. Like the stream that bends to sea,

Like the pine that seeks the blue, Minnesota, still for thee, Thy sons are strong and true. From thy woods and waters fair,

From thy prairies waving far, At thy call they throng, With their shout and song, Hailing thee their Northern Star.

* excerpted

The American Swedish Institute in Minneapolis is a museum and cultural center.

Celebrating Culture

F rench Canadians and people from Sweden, Norway, Germany, and Ireland were some of Minnesota's first settlers of European heritage. They were soon joined by immigrants from Finland, Poland, and what are now the Czech Republic and Slovakia. A number of different ethnic festivals are held throughout the state each year.

In April, St. Paul hosts a celebration of the state's ethnic diversity with the Festival of Nations. Visitors to the annual Immigrants' Christmas, held in Annandale's Minnesota Pioneer Park, can learn about the holiday traditions of many of the state's ethnic groups.

The major areas of Swedish settlement in the state are immediately north of the Twin Cities and in scattered locations in west-central and northwestern Minnesota. The American Swedish Institute, in Minneapolis, runs a museum about the area's Swedish heritage. Traditional Swedish fiddling, dancing, folk costumes, crafts, games, and food are all part of the many festivals that the institute sponsors throughout the year.

Several Native American groups in Minnesota hold annual powwows that feature drumming and different styles of Native American dancing. In September, a public powwow by the Dakota at Mankato celebrates their traditional ways. The annual powwow in Hinckley attracts Native Americans from all over the Midwest.

The Scandinavian Hjemkomst Festival celebrates the cultures of Finland, Denmark, Iceland, Norway, and Sweden. The festival takes place in mid to late June each year.

The Leech Lake powwows happen several times throughout the spring, summer, and fall. They feature the cultural dress and dance of the Ojibwe Native Americans.

Arts and Entertainment

The Twin Cities area serves as the center of Minnesota's cultural institutions. The Minnesota Orchestra performs in Orchestra Hall in downtown Minneapolis. The hall is famous for the **acoustic** cubes on its ceiling and stage walls. These cubes deflect the sound throughout the hall so that the audience can hear the performance perfectly. The Minnesota Dance Theatre is the most prominent resident dance company in the Twin Cities. The famous Guthrie Theater opened in Minneapolis in 1963. It is named after Sir Tyrone Guthrie, a British stage director and actor, who helped establish the theater company. There are many art galleries in Minnesota. Perhaps the best known is the Walker Art Center in Minneapolis, which opened in 1927, and since the 1940s, has focused on modern art.

Chanhassan Dinner Theater, in Minneapolis, is the **largest dinner theater** in the country.

The first **children's** area in a library was created in the **Minneapolis Public Library** in 1889.

Born in Minneapolis, Minnesota, James Arness was best known for his 20-year role of Marshal Matt Dillon on *Gunsmoke*.

Many famous entertainers have come from Minnesota. They include James Arness, who starred in the TV Show *Gunsmoke*, and Judy Garland, who starred in films such as *The Wizard of Oz, Meet Me in St. Louis,* and *A Star Is Born*. More recent stars from Minnesota include Ethan and Joel Coen, who together write, direct, and produce films. Singer and songwriter Bob Dylan was born in Duluth and raised in Hibbing.

Numerous writers call Minnesota home. They include Sinclair Lewis, F. Scott Fitzgerald, Louis Erdrich, and children's author Maud Hart Lovelace, whose books were based on her own life growing up in Mankato. Garrison Keillor, who writes about life in the imaginary Lake Wobegon, was host to the popular radio program called *A Prairie Home Companion*.

Judy Garland grew up in Grand Rapids, Minnesota. She began her career as a child, singing and dancing with her sisters.

The Grammy Award-winning Minnesota Orchestra has been performing for more than 100 years.

Sports and Recreation

The Twin Cities boast five major professional sports teams in four different sports. The Minnesota Vikings play in the National Football League. The Minnesota Twins, who play in baseball's American League, have twice won the World Series, in 1987 and 1991. There are currently two professional basketball teams, the Timberwolves in the National Basketball Association and the Lynx in the Women's National Basketball Association. The Minnesota Wild have competed in the National Hockey League since 2000.

The first modern **water skis** were first tested on a lake in Lake City, Minnesota, in 1922.

More than half of the players on the 1980 U.S. Olympic Men's Hockey Team, known as the **"MIRACLE ON ICE,"** were born in Minnesota.

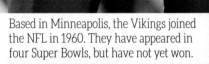

Based in Minneapolis, the Vikings joined the NFL in 1960. They have appeared in four Super Bowls, but have not yet won.

High schools, colleges, and universities throughout the state have very active sports programs. The Golden Gophers sports teams of the University of Minnesota have won national championships over the years in various sports, including football, baseball, wrestling, and both men's and women's ice hockey.

With so many well-stocked lakes and streams in the state, Minnesotans never run out of places to fish. The many bodies of water offer other activities as well, such as waterskiing, kayaking, canoeing, motorboating, and inner-tubing. Popular winter sports in Minnesota include skiing, snowboarding, snowmobiling, snowshoeing, and dog sledding. Minnesota is the envy of

The Minnesota Timberwolves play all of their home games at the Target Center in Minneapolis. They have made the playoffs eight years in a row without making it to the championship.

the nation when it comes to cross-country ski and snowmobile trails. The largest and highest downhill ski area in the Midwest is found at Spirit Mountain, near Duluth.

Named after the Twin Cities of St. Paul and Minneapolis, the Minnesota Twins moved to the area from Washington, D.C., in 1960.

Get To Know MINNESOTA

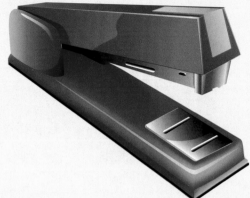

The **stapler** was invented in Spring Valley, Minnesota.

Minnesota ranks first in the U.S. for highest percentage of residents with fishing licenses.

The Minneapolis Sculpture Garden is the **largest sculpture garden in the country.**

The **SPAM©** Museum in Austin is dedicated to the mystery pork product that is cooked in the can it comes in.

The Mall of America, in Bloomington, is the largest mall in the United States. It is the size of **78 football fields**.

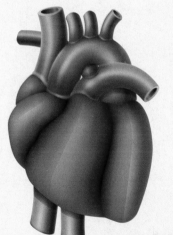

The first successful **open heart surgery** ever performed happened at the University of Minnesota in 1952.

At **2,301 feet**, Eagle Mountain is the highest point in Minnesota.

Brain Teasers

What have you learned about Minnesota after reading this book? Test your knowledge by answering these questions. All of the information can be found in the text you just read. The answers are provided below for easy reference.

1 What is the capital of Minnesota?

2 Which cereal company is headquartered in Minnesota?

3 Who were the first Europeans to visit Minnesota?

4 What is the name of the April festival in St. Paul that celebrates Minnesota's ethnic diversity?

5 When did the Native Americans of the Ojibwe and Chippewa migrate into what is now Minnesota?

6 In what year did Minnesota become a state?

7 Which Minnesota native starred in *The Wizard of Oz* movie?

8 What does Minneapolis mean?

ANSWER KEY
1. St. Paul 2. General Mills 3. Pierre Esprit Radisson and Médard Chouart 4. Festival of Nations 5. The late 1600s 6. 1858 7. Judy Garland 8. City of Water

Key Words

acoustic: of or relating to sound or hearing

barges: flat-bottomed boats used on canals and rivers to carry goods

bogs: areas of wet, spongy ground

coniferous forests: forests with primarily cone-bearing and needle-leaved trees

cooperatives: businesses owned by their members with profits shared between them

deciduous forests: forests with primarily broad-leaved trees that lose their leaves every year

First Amendment: an amendment to the U.S. Constitution that protects freedom of religion, speech, assembly, or petition

flour milling: grinding and sifting wheat, rye, and other grains into flour for making bread and cakes

glaciers: large masses of slow-moving ice

metropolitan area: a city and its surrounding suburbs and towns

migrated: moved from one place to another

open-pit mines: huge holes in the ground where minerals are mined, loaded into trucks, and hauled away for processing

species: a group of animals or plants that share the same characteristics and can mate

Index

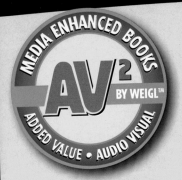

Log on to www.av2books.com

AV² by Weigl brings you media enhanced books that support active learning. Go to www.av2books.com, and enter the special code found on page 2 of this book. You will gain access to enriched and enhanced content that supplements and complements this book. Content includes video, audio, weblinks, quizzes, a slide show, and activities.

AV² Online Navigation

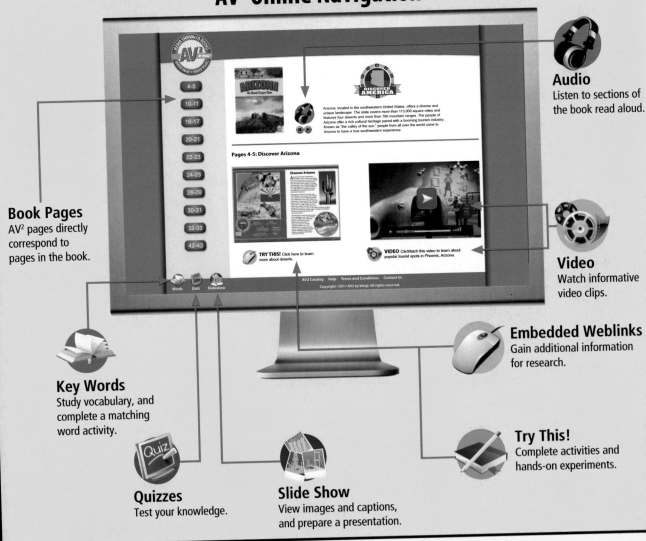

Audio
Listen to sections of the book read aloud.

Book Pages
AV² pages directly correspond to pages in the book.

Video
Watch informative video clips.

Embedded Weblinks
Gain additional information for research.

Key Words
Study vocabulary, and complete a matching word activity.

Try This!
Complete activities and hands-on experiments.

Quizzes
Test your knowledge.

Slide Show
View images and captions, and prepare a presentation.

AV² was built to bridge the gap between print and digital. We encourage you to tell us what you like and what you want to see in the future.

Sign up to be an AV² Ambassador at www.av2books.com/ambassador.

Due to the dynamic nature of the Internet, some of the URLs and activities provided as part of AV² by Weigl may have changed or ceased to exist. AV² by Weigl accepts no responsibility for any such changes. All media enhanced books are regularly monitored to update addresses and sites in a timely manner. Contact AV² by Weigl at 1-866-649-3445 or av2books@weigl.com with any questions, comments, or feedback.